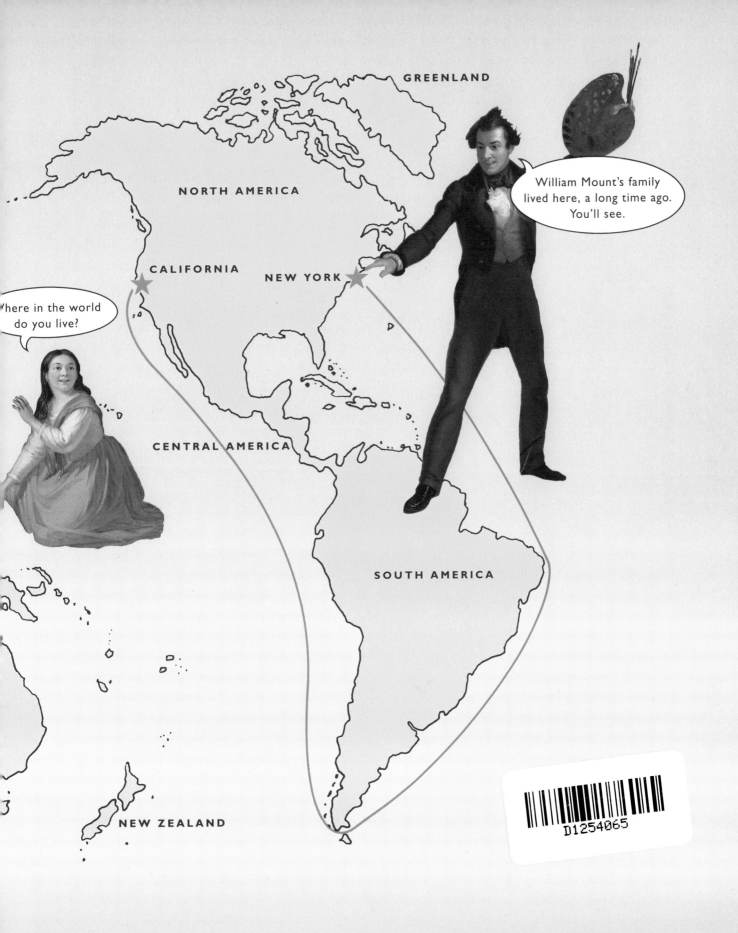

William Sidney Mount

Painter of Rural America

Nancy Shroyer Howard

A CLOSER LOOK
ACTIVITY BOOK

I'll wait for you on page 18.

Davis Publications, Inc.
Worcester, Massachusetts

For our boys, Bill and Malcolm, and for everyone's children.

Acknowledgments

With gratitude to The Museums at Stony Brook, whose incomparable Mount collection and energetic outreach to the public were inspirations for this book.

With gratitude, also, to the dedicated museum educators at The Museums at Stony Brook and at the Museum of Fine Arts, Boston, with whom ways of introducing art to children were developed over the years. And to Martha Siegel, Wyatt Wade and Susan Marsh, for turning these ways into this book.

Warm thanks to teachers, museum colleagues and artists who reviewed the drafts, improved them and lent support: Deborah Johnson, Bill Burback, Lorri Berenberg, Sally Leahy, Helen Neumeyer, Alice Proctor, Merr Shearn and, most especially, Richard Mello.

Editor: Martha Philippa Siegel
Design: Susan Marsh

Library of Congress Catalog Card Number: 93–72834
ISBN: 87192–275–4   10 9 8 7 6 5 4 3 2 1
Printed in Korea

Cover: *The Novice*, 1847. Oil on canvas, 30" x 25" (76 cm x 64 cm). The Museums at Stony Brook, New York.

Let's Go!

Meet William Sidney Mount (1807–1868), one of the finest and best known artists living during the middle of the 1800s in the United States of America.

This book takes you into his time as he saw, lived and pictured it. Along the way, you will meet William Mount's two brothers, Henry and Shepard, also artists. We'll use first names to avoid confusion.

(For more information about the Mounts, turn to page 46.)

In this book, you will find three types of activities for exploring each of William Mount's paintings:

1. Quick activities are first, in big letters like this.
   ■ Look for the red squares to guide you.

2. Further explorations come next, in smaller letters.
   ■ Look for the gold squares to guide you.

3. **Projects going deeper are in little letters like this.**
   ■ **Look for the green squares to guide you.**

Do as much or as little as you like.
Relax.
Have a good time.

(For a list of museums where you can see the original drawings and paintings that appear in this book, turn to the inside back cover.)

William Sidney Mount grew up on a farm on Long Island, New York. New York City was a day away by sailboat or stagecoach. William probably looked like this boy.
←

To see what's going on here, turn the page. →

William Mount
called his painting
Catching Crabs or
Spearing Crabs.

What is everyone doing?

▨ To get the picture, find the different parts →
in this painting of a Long Island farm scene.

calling to a
little girl in the
farmhouse

cutting salt hay
for the cows
to eat

returning home
after fishing

pulling hay into
the barn

carrying
cornmeal home
from the mill

catching crabs
for dinner

■ It takes lots of hard work to keep a farm going. Yet William made this painting look very peaceful.

Name some ways that he made this scene seem peaceful. Look it over from top to bottom, side to side.

Are any of your ideas like these? Or better? ↓

- A group of buildings on the right side of the painting balances the building on the left side.
- Buildings and shoreline form a straight, steady line across the painting.
- There is no tipping over, no fighting, no trouble.
- There are soft, gentle colors.
- Are there other things you notice: the water? the sky?

■ **Action please!**

Change the scene. As soon as a crab is speared, it has to be flipped into the boy's basket, or *creel*. With another person, act out the man and boy sneaking up on the crab.

(There is a lot of mud under that water, so slip around. The mud is sticky, so add sound effects.)

Flip the crab into the basket without getting pinched. Make waves.

Now, look again and imagine how Mount's picture would look if he had painted your wild scene.

William Mount loved fishing and boating.

He painted this skillful woman teaching a boy the tricky art of spearing from a boat. When William was a boy, he learned spearing from a man named Hector. Mount wrote:

An old Negro named Hector gave me the first lesson in spearing flat-fish, and eels. Early one morning we were along shore . . . it was calm, and the water was as clear as a mirror . . . now and then could be seen an eel darting through the seaweed, or a flatfish shifting his place and throwing the sand over his body for safty . . . "Stop the boat," shouts Hector, "shove a little back, more to the left . . . don't you see those eyes, how they shine like diamonds" . . . and away went his iron and the clear bottom was nothing but a cloud of moving sand . . . . That fish proved to be a large flounder, and the way old Hector shouted was a caution to all wind instruments."

■ Suspense!

In this painting, William begins a story. Will the woman see a fish to spear? What will happen next?

Finish the story your way: "Suddenly the woman sees a flatfish half buried in the sandy bottom of the harbor. Swiftly she jabs the spear into the water. Then . . . ." (You finish it.)

Oh, Oh!
Not everyone is working here!

The boys have thrown their pitchforks down.
It's much too hot and sunny to pitch hay in the fields.
It's much nicer to loaf in the dark shadow of the trees.

■ Who's napping? Waking up? Daydreaming? Sneaking up?

■ What do you suppose each person is thinking? Or dreaming?

■ On paper, draw yourself working somewhere. Then draw yourself goofing off and being caught.

William Mount called this painting *Boys Caught Napping in a Field*.

Now here's a picture that could wake up anybody!

With a ring in its nose a pig can't root or dig a hole under the fence with its snout and run away.

William Mount called this painting *Ringing the Pig* or *Scene in a Long Island Farm Yard*.

■ Imagine that you jump into the pigpen. Imagine these sounds:
- a scared pig squealing.
- a little boy squealing.
- a big boy swinging a cornstalk.
- pigs grumbling and munching.

Imagine that a storm is coming. Add the sounds of a storm. Don't forget:
- wind through the trees.
- the roof of the pig shed blowing off.
- pigs running scared.

If you have a tape cassette recorder, find other people and record sounds, first one at a time then all together, for a whirlwind farm chorus.

■ Before William painted *Ringing the Pig* he tried out his ideas in this drawing, a study for the painting. →

Find the ideas that Mount decided to change when he painted the final ← picture.

Why do you think he changed these things?

(For more action? Color?)

How do you like the way he painted pigs?

■ Draw quick pencil studies of yourself in a farm scene. Try different ideas, as William did. Then take the ideas you like best and turn them into a picture in color.

Here's a BIG farm scene.

William Mount called it *Cider Making*. Have you ever drunk cider made from squashed apples?

■ Play a memory game.

First look at how William arranged the whole painting. Let your eyes make a big circle around the scene.

Next look at every small part (detail) from side to side.

Then close your eyes and try to remember where William put each part.

Got it?
Now turn the page. →

Now test your memory.

Here is a study that William Mount drew before he painted *Cider Making*.

■ Do you remember where he put each of these characters in his final painting? ↓

Point to where they belong in William's drawing. →

the horse that powers the wheel that crushes the apples

extra weight on the turning wheel

man who catches the cider at the spout and pours it into barrels

driver of the apple-crusher

man who presses the juicy cider from crushed apples

cider taster

recyclers of leftovers

cider snitchers

How's your memory?
Do you want to
turn back and check?

William worked
hard to arrange
(compose)
his paintings.
How would *you*
compose this scene?
Point to where you
would put each of his
characters.

Turn yourself into an
Apple Cider Freak.

On paper plan your own
Cider Making composition.

Invent a fantastic cider
machine.

Add your friends working
and snitching.

Shepard Mount drew a quick sketch of his brother William painting *Cider Making*.

■ What part of the painting is William working on? →

■ In Shepard's sketch, find a few zigzag lines drawn quickly, some strong, straight lines, and other lighter, crossed lines.

Point to spots where the lines make dark places, then light gray places to show the roundness of William's body.

How does Shepard show that the light is coming from behind William?

And William drew a picture of Shepard.

■ William took his time. The lines he drew are very different from Shepard's lines. →

Find words that describe the lines William used for face and hair. Then find words for the lines Shepard used.

On pieces of paper, draw heads. Experiment with lines — zigzag, curved, straight, thick, thin, light, dark and crossed.

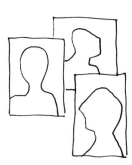

William liked to paint barns, sometimes full of trouble.

Oh, oh.
What is it this time?

This painting has two names, *Truant Gamblers* and *The Undutiful Boys*.

But usually
William filled his barns
with music!

William Mount was crazy about music. He played the violin and liked to dance.

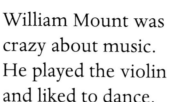

■ Right now, his neighbors are warming up. Who is:
• drumming a rhythm?
• playing a melody?
• slapping his knee?
• dancing the hornpipe, a sailors' dance?

These are the music-makers William painted in one of his barn pictures. To see how William showed variety in his painting, take the pose of each person here.

■ William sketched several ideas (studies) for dances. Find the music-makers that are most like his sketches.

Then, turn the page to see how William's ideas worked out. →

This is the finished painting, *Dance of the Haymakers.*

Work is done for the day.
Everyone is having a good time.

■ Find the places where Mount decided
to put each music-maker.
←

■ Is there anyone else here
who could be making music?
• Singing?
• Whistling?
• Foot-tapping?
• Howling?

■ Point to who is outside the barn, closest to you.
Who is just inside the barn?
Who is further inside the barn?

William learned to show what looked close and what looked far away in a painting.

How could he show deep space when paintings are flat?

 With your hand, trace the boards in the barn.

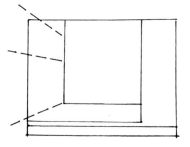

Follow how they slant toward each other. This makes the boards look like they go way back in space.

(Good trick?)

■ Do the dark colors inside the barn make the building look even deeper? ← →

See if light colors make the grass and pitchfork look closer than the girls in the hayloft. ← →

If the girls are tiny ↑ and the boy is big, → who looks farther away in space?

If the fiddler is higher from the bottom of the picture than the dog, who looks ↗ farther away? ↓

If the man's legs block out part of the boy, ↑ who looks farther back?

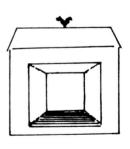

■ Try out Mount's ideas.

On a big piece of paper, draw a barn with deep space. Add yourself and your friends, up close and far away, having a barn party. Don't forget to add good things to eat.

So, William Mount created space (perspective) by:

- **making lines slant toward each other,**
- **making far things smaller and sometimes darker,**
- **having near things overlap farther things,**
- **putting farther things higher in the picture.**

William created even deeper space in *Dancing on the Barn Floor.* →

How did he do it?

■ Show how the slanted boards in this painting make the barn look deep.

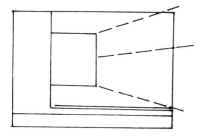

Measure how tall each girl is. See how William made one girl tiny to look very far back in the barn.

Then see how William leads your eyes even farther back in space — right out the back door and into the trees.

■ See how William used overlapping. The horse ↑ covers up part of the post. So, which one is farther away, the horse or the post?

The fiddler's arm → overlaps the barn door. So, which is closer to you?

See where William placed each character. Whose feet are placed lowest and whose are highest in the painting? Who is closest to you, slightly farther, farther still and farthest away?

(The two dancers' feet are almost the same, but look carefully at where they touch the floor.)

■ Have some perspective!

Fold a long, stiff piece of paper in thirds, to look like the inside of a barn. On cardboard or strong paper draw musicians, dancers, animals and farm tools. Make some big, some small. Draw a flap at the bottom of each one so it can stand. Cut each one out. Fold the flaps back. Arrange the figures in the barn. Try many different ways — up front, far back, overlapping — until the perspective looks right to you. →

24

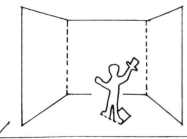

William Mount also painted close-ups of people.

These close-up paintings are called *portraits*.

Here are musicians William knew. He probably played his violin with them and danced to their music.

These three portraits are called *Just in Tune, The Banjo Player* and *Right and Left*.

■ Guess which is which.

Answer:

At the top of this page is *Right and Left*, a left-handed fiddler.

Below is *Just in Tune*, tuning up.

On the next page is *The Banjo Player*.

How did you do?

■ Play a game.

William showed how each musician looks different and special.

On three small pieces of paper, write five words that describe each musician.

See if anyone can guess which words belong to which musician.

■ William used color to make each portrait life-like and lively.

With your hands:

• Show where William changed the color on the face of *The Banjo Player* to make it look rounded, real, alive. →

• Show where William used red paint here and there to lead your eyes all around *The Banjo Player* in a lively way. →

William Mount's portraits became famous.
You can almost hear the music.

He called this portrait *The Bone Player*.
←

■ Make a fast rhythm like *The Bone Player* does. Click old, dry bones, spoons or blocks, slap your knee, or clap your hands.

Get a good rhythm going. Add a tune. Hum, whistle, sing, dance. Then FREEZE!
Choose some good poses for portraits.

■ William planned *Just in Tune*, *The Banjo Player*, *Right and Left* and *The Bone Player* as close-ups.
(Look, no legs.)

This makes the hands and musical instruments important, right?

Plan a portrait of a musician you've seen. Choose the instrument, the pose, what to include and what to leave out.

Try out ideas in quick sketches on paper. Then draw or paint the portrait as best you can.
(People can be hard to picture.)

■ Here are three whole portraits in *The Novice*.
Find ways that each boy is individual or unique.
(That's what makes good portraits.)

Maybe William Mount looked like this boy when he was a beginner, or novice, on the flute.
(Look at William's self-portrait on page 31 for proof that he liked the flute.)

William copied down songs he wanted to play. Try to sing or play "The Arkansas Traveler." ↓

William's brother Shepard was a fine portrait painter too.

This is Shepard's portrait of Tutie, his daughter.

To show what Tutie was like and what was important to her, Shepard added special things, called attributes.

Notice what Tutie wears and what she holds in her hands and apron.

←

Shepard Mount called this portrait *Rose of Sharon,* the flower Tutie holds.

William painted William.

When William Mount was twenty-one years old he painted his first portrait of himself, a self-portrait.
←

■ How did Mount show what was important to him?
• What is he holding?
• What is he wearing?
• How did he pose?
• What about his look?

■ When William was twenty-five, he painted another self-portrait.
↙

Point to places where William's way of painting himself changed after four years. Do you like one portrait more than the other? Because . . . ?

■ Plan a portrait of yourself. Think over a few ideas:
• What is your pose?
• What are you doing?
• What are you holding?
• What is your outfit?
• Are you alone? Is there a big audience?

Make your self-portrait in bits and pieces, a collage. Show places, people and things you like. On paper or cardboard, arrange cut-outs from magazines, pieces of fabric, yarn, aluminum foil, bottle caps, labels, stickers and photos — whatever shows what *you* are like.

Artists like the Mounts practiced ways of making people look real, alive.

■ Figure out which of these details belongs to each portrait: ←
→
↓

- *Just in Tune*
- *Right and Left*
- *The Novice*
- *Rose of Sharon*
- *Self Portrait with Flute*
- *The Banjo Player*
- *The Bone Player*

Surprise! Here is another portrait by William Mount.

→
This painting is called *Esquimaux Dog*.

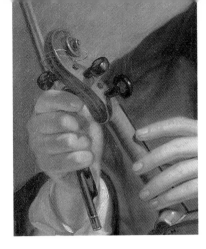

Turn back to the portraits on pages 26, 27, 28, 29, 30 and 31. Decide whether these details make the portraits seem alive.

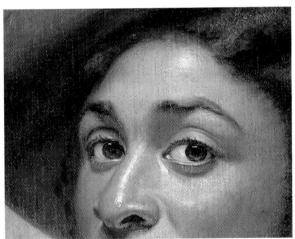

Look at each of these details again. Describe how the Mounts used white and light-colored paint to show glowing skin, rounded fingers, bright eyes, shiny nails and sparkling glass.

33

William Mount often added small details to make a picture interesting, full of things to look at and think about.

picnic lunch

water's edge

tool box

■ Remember these details?
← Find them again in their paintings. See if the details make the pictures more fun to look at.

■ Details can be like little paintings themselves. Look back through this book for details you like.

Hold your hands like this. →
Discover details that make fine pictures by themselves.

See life standing still.

Paintings of objects, not people, are called *still-life paintings*. Here are two examples by William Mount's brothers, Henry and Shepard.

Henry Smith Mount's still life is called *Vase of Flowers.* →

■ **Count the different kinds of flowers and leaves Henry put together to make this wild, interesting still life. In the painting find three kinds of leaves or flowers. Draw each one to show how its special shape, color and size add something different to the still life.** (This takes careful looking.)

Shepard Alonzo Mount's still life is called *Fish.*

←

Shepard shows how the scales of his fish catch the light and glow in many colors. Arrange three shiny things (glass, metal, foil, fish?) into a still-life composition you like. Make a colorful picture that shows how each object catches light and color.

(This is a hard one.)

35

Have you noticed that William and Shepard liked to paint the land where they lived?

These paintings are called landscapes.

Go hiking.

Let your eyes:
• walk out of the house
• sit below a tree
• crawl under the wagon
• run over the pasture to the opening in the forest

Stop.
Name the colors William used to show you:
• the season
• the time of day
• the weather

Study the clouds, the darkening sky and the shadows.
Hunt for the best picnic spot on a day like this.

Go fishing.

Shepard painted landscapes that just pull you in.
Remember the painting of Tutie on page 30?
Let your eyes:
• run in front of Tutie
• jump over the clump of grass
• dive into the pond
• climb onto the rocks
• swing a net through the water
• dash to the house to cook your fish

Sometimes William made quick sketches outdoors.

He wrote notes about the colors he saw ↑
so he wouldn't forget what they were.
Then he went indoors, into his studio,
to paint the scene.

■ Try it.

Take paper, pencils and a board or
something to press on. Go outdoors.
Look around.

Sketch a landscape with trees,
flowers, sky or whatever is out there
that you like. Sometimes William
cheated and added mountains!
(See some there?)
Feel free to exaggerate.

Sketch a cityscape or townscape with
trucks, fire hydrants, stores, houses or
a spaceship landing.

Sketch a seascape or a mud-puddle-
scape with flat or wavy water, boats,
swimming creatures, maybe a whale.

Write notes about the colors on your
sketches. Go inside. Turn your
sketches into colorful pictures.

Of course, Mount also worked indoors.

You can see that he wrote reminders all over this quick sketch of his kitchen. ↖
This is a kitchen? Sure.

▇ In this sketch ↑ find the up-to-date 1840s appliances:

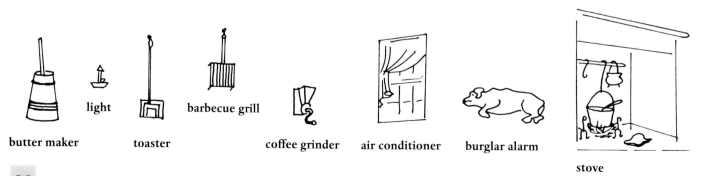

butter maker   light   toaster   barbecue grill   coffee grinder   air conditioner   burglar alarm

stove

William Mount called this painting *Artist Showing His Own Work* or *The Painter's Triumph.* ↓

■ Here Mount celebrated the artist at work, full of excitement and pride. Look for ways that William created this mood. See if your ideas are anything like these:

- The farmer crouches and looks closely at the painting.
- Like a hero, the artist raises his palette and brushes.
- The artist places his feet dramatically, one foot pointing toward the easel.
- The artist's hand points to a special spot in the painting.
- The artist's eyes are fixed on that spot.
- The farmer grins. He must like it, too.

■ Let the painting talk.

What would the artist and farmer be saying? Write a short play or story:
- the farmer drives up to William's house in his horse and wagon,
- he ties his horse to a tree outside,
- still holding his horse whip, the farmer climbs up to William's studio,
- to talk about a painting of . . . ?

The name of this painting is *Crane Neck Across the Marsh*.

You'll never guess where William found colors for his paints.

Would you believe that William and Shepard Mount climbed the cliff in the distance → to gather colors from the earth?

What colors can you spot on the sandy beach ↑ and cliff?

Here is what William wrote about digging for colors:

My brother S. A. Mount proposed that we should explore the high banks . . .
to see what we could find in the way of native [local] pigments [colors] . . . .
We picked up pieces of brown, yellow, and . . . Shepard struck his hoe a few feet
up the bank and we were astonished to see a lot of bright red running down the
bank and mingling with the sand. It was a rich day for us . . . some of these
sandstone balls contained purple, some yellow, and some red, like orange
vermillion . . . . About seventy feet above tide water, we dug out a white powder
encased in a covering so slight that . . . we were obliged to take the powder
out with a spoon.

From Mount's letter to Benjamin Thompson, 1848

▪ The Mount brothers ground to a fine powder the pigments
(colored minerals) they found on the cliff. They mixed the powders with
liquids to make either watercolor paint or oil paint.

These are some of the paint colors William and Shepard used. →
← Look back through this book and search for these earth colors in the
Mounts' paintings.

In his journal William showed how he laid blobs of paint on his palette
before he began a picture. He used both earth colors and store-bought
colors, like blue. How many of these brushstrokes of paint →
can you find on William's picture of his palette? ↙

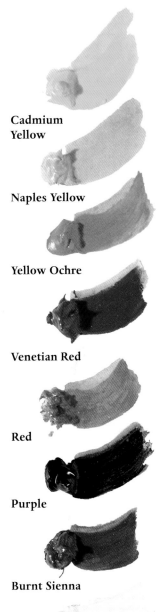

Cadmium
Yellow

Naples Yellow

Yellow Ochre

Venetian Red

Red

Purple

Burnt Sienna

Flake White

Terre Verte

Ivory Black

▪ **Go exploring.**

Search for earth colors in:
- **mud, clay,**
- **vegetables, fruit,**
- **grasses, leaves.**

**On paper, draw a painter's
palette. Rub samples of
your colors onto the
palette. See if any of your
colors are like William
Mount's earth colors.**

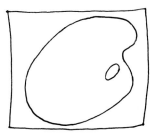

More About William Sidney Mount

William Sidney Mount was born in 1807 and died in 1867.

William Sidney Mount lived in the small seaside village of Stony Brook on Long Island, 50 miles from New York City. At that time, the United States was still quite young. The U.S. Constitution went into effect only nineteen years before William was born.

William grew up in a family of artists. As a boy he watched his sister Ruth's painting lessons. "Then you could have seen me looking over my sister's shoulder, with my straw hat in hand, to see how she put on the colours." At age seventeen, William became an apprentice to his brother, Henry Smith Mount, a sign and ornamental painter in New York City.

One day William visited an exhibition of paintings, "the first collection I ever had the pleasure of seeing. As I ascended the stairs, the sight of so many pictures in rich frames, the figures the size of life looking upon me from all parts of the room, created a strange bewilderment . . . my mind was awakened to a new life and big resolves for the future were then made."

William became one of the first students at the National Academy of Design when it opened in New York. In 1829, William and his brother, Shepard Alonzo Mount, opened shop together in New York City. "(We) set up our easels for chance customers. Our notification to the public was 'W. S. and S. A. Mount, portrait painters.' "

Throughout the middle of the 1800s, William became well known in the United States and Europe as one of the first and finest painters of everyday rural life in the young nation. Although William visited New York City and kept in touch with the work of other artists, he chose to live on Long Island to paint its people, their farming, fishing, music and humor. The growing number of people who lived in congested cities welcomed William's pictures of country life.

William Mount painted people of all kinds, young and old, white and black, farmers, dancers, fisherwomen and musicians. Usually they lived nearby. William Mount was one of the first American painters to depict African Americans with individuality and dignity. The African American farm workers and musicians you see in his paintings were not slaves. Slavery had been outlawed in New York State in 1827.

Life in the United States was changing fast in William's time. People, industries and cities were spreading across the land. Steam-powered ships and trains carried families, supplies and ideas farther and more quickly than ever before. Gold was discovered in California. It was a breathtaking time.

Yet William traveled neither west to seek his fortune nor to Europe to study the great paintings of England, France and Italy. "It has always been my desire to see the old masters," he wrote, "but I still feel there is something yet to be learned at home." Like the poets Ralph Waldo Emerson and Walt Whitman, William preferred to celebrate the America he knew, admired and loved. Because he did it so well, William Sidney Mount himself is celebrated today as the earliest major painter of everyday rural life in the U.S.A.

Long Island is rich in character. It would be worth the trouble to stay a short time in each village. A painter's studio should be every where, wherever he finds a scene for a picture in doors or out — In the black smith's shop, the shoe maker's, the tailor's, the church, the tavern, or Hotel, the market, and into the dens of poverty and dissipation, high life and low life. In the full blaze of the sun, in moonlight and shadow. Then on the wave, the sea shore, in the cottage by fire light and at the theatre. See the sun rise and set. Go and search for materials, not waiting for them to come to you. Attend Fairs, shows, campmeetings and horse racings . . . an artist should have the industry of a reporter.

— William Sidney Mount

46

Visiting the Mounts' Drawings and Paintings

Wouldn't it be wonderful to see the Mounts' pictures, the originals? There's nothing like seeing the real colors and brushstrokes of paint. Here is where you can find the drawings and paintings that appear in this book.

The Novice, 1847. Oil on canvas, 30" x 25" (76 cm x 64 cm). The Museums at Stony Brook, New York. Museums Purchase, 1962.

Catching Crabs (Spearing Crabs), 1865. Oil on canvas, 18¼" x 24¼" (46 cm x 62 cm). The Museums at Stony Brook, New York. Gift of Mr. and Mrs. Ward Melville, 1958.

Eel Spearing at Setauket (Fishing Along Shore), 1845. Oil on canvas, 28½" x 36" (72 cm x 91 cm). The New York State Historical Association, Cooperstown, New York.

Turning the Leaf (Surprise with Admiration), 1848. Oil on panel, 12¾" x 17" (33 cm x 43 cm). The Museums at Stony Brook, New York. Gift of Mr. and Mrs. Ward Melville, 1958.

Maybe I'll be able to play this by the time I see you again.

Boy Hoeing Corn, 1840. Oil on panel, 15" x 11½" (38 cm x 29 cm). The Museums at Stony Brook, New York. Gift of Mr. and Mrs. Ward Melville, 1955.

Boys Caught Napping in a Field (Caught Napping), 1848. Oil on canvas, 29" x 36⅛" (74 cm x 92 cm). The Brooklyn Museum, New York. Dick S. Ramsay Fund.

Ringing the Pig (Scene in a Long Island Farm Yard), 1842. Oil on canvas, 26" x 30" (66 cm x 76 cm). The New York State Historical Association, Cooperstown, New York.

Sketch for *Ringing the Pig,* about 1842. Pencil on paper, 9" x 13½" (23 cm x 34 cm). The Museums at Stony Brook, New York. Bequest of Mr. Ward Melville, 1977.

Cider Making, 1841. Oil on canvas, 27" x 34⅛" (69 cm x 86 cm). The Metropolitan Museum of Art, New York. Charles Allen Munn Bequest.

Study for *Cider Making,* about 1841. Pencil on paper, 6¹¹⁄₁₆" x 13⅜" (17 cm x 34 cm). The Museums at Stony Brook, New York. Bequest of Mr. Ward Melville, 1977.

Shepard Alonzo Mount, *William Sidney Mount Painting Cider Making,* 1841. Pencil on paper, 8½" x 7½" (22 cm x 19 cm). The Museums at Stony Brook, New York. Museums Collection.

Portrait of Shepard Alonzo Mount, no date. Pencil on paper, 9⁵⁄₁₆" x 7³⁄₁₆" (23 cm x 20 cm). The Museums at Stony Brook, New York. Gift of Mrs. John Slade, in memory of her aunt, Mrs. Sarah C. W. Hoppin, 1957.

The Truant Gamblers (Undutiful Boys), 1835. Oil on canvas, 24" x 30" (61 cm x 76 cm). The New York Historical Society, New York.

Detail from *Study for Dance of the Haymakers and The Power of Music,* about 1845. Pencil on paper, 9" x 5½" (23 cm x 14 cm). The Museums at Stony Brook, New York. Bequest of Mr. Ward Melville, 1977.

Two details from *Sheet of Sketches,* 1866. Pencil on paper, 12½" x 8" (32 cm x 20 cm). The Museums at Stony Brook, New York. Bequest of Mrs. Scott Kidder, 1956.

Dance of the Haymakers (Music is Contagious), 1845. Oil on canvas, 24" x 29" (61 cm x 74 cm). The Museums at Stony Brook, New York. Gift of Mr. and Mrs. Ward Melville, 1950.

Dancing on the Barn Floor (Interior of a Barn with Figures), 1831. Oil on canvas, 24⅝" x 29⅝" (63 cm x 75 cm). The